BookLife

JOHN FARNDON

THE

SUN
AND STARS
OTHER

EXPLORING THE UNIVERSE

INTRODUCTION

Have you ever looked at the awesome stars in the night sky and wondered how they shine? The Sun is our star. It gives us light and heat, but do you know how old it is or how it was born?

This book will propel you into space to explore the Sun and all the stars. Discover what happens during an eclipse, find out why stars seem to twinkle and learn all about the brightest stars. This book will teach you everything you need to know about the stars, and much more.

SPOT
&
COUNT!

WATCH OUT FOR THESE CIRCLES TO LEARN MORE ABOUT THE TRULY WEIRD AND WONDERFUL FACTS ABOUT SPACE AND THE UNIVERSE IN WHICH WE LIVE. ★

FACT FOCUS

SPACE BITS

Look out for these boxes to take a closer look at space features.

ZOOM

Q: Why watch out for these boxes?

★ ★

A: They give answers to the space questions you always wanted to ask.

Q & A

THIS EDITION:
2015 © BOOK LIFE
KING'S LYNN
PE30 4HG

FIRST PUBLISHED:
2001©ALADDIN BOOKS LTD
PO BOX 53987
LONDON SW15 2SF

ISBN: 978-1-910512-19-7

A CATALOGUE RECORD FOR THIS BOOK IS AVAILABLE FROM THE BRITISH LIBRARY.

PRINTED: MALAYSIA

DESIGNED BY:
IAN McMULLEN

EDITED BY:
GRACE JONES

STARGAZING

When you look into the sky on a clear night you will see thousands of stars. You cannot see them in the daytime since the sky is too bright, but they are still there. The star groups do not change, which makes it easy to learn your way around. You can study the stars with the naked eye, with binoculars or with a telescope. Never look directly at the Sun.

FACT FOCUS

THE STARS ARE HUGE. THE SMALLEST STAR IS ONE HUNDRED TIMES LARGER THAN JUPITER, THE LARGEST PLANET IN OUR SOLAR SYSTEM.

★

You do not need any equipment to study the stars. With the naked eye alone you can see the Milky Way, watch for shooting stars or pick out some of the main star groups.

Looking through binoculars, the Milky Way becomes thousands of individual stars. Some brighter galaxies show up as fuzzy light. You can see more clearly the difference in colour and brightness of individual stars.

Looking with a telescope, you can see even more detail. You can see craters on the Moon and the rings of Saturn. You can also see clouds of dust and gas, like the Orion nebula, just below Orion's belt, where stars are being born.

WITH THE NAKED EYE YOU CAN SEE ABOUT 2,000 STARS!

OUR AMAZING SUN

The Sun is a star, and like all stars it is a huge fiery ball. The temperature at the centre of the Sun reaches over 15 million °C! The Sun is much hotter than any fire on Earth, and is hot enough to melt any known substance. Inside the Sun one kind of gas is changing into another. This is what makes it shine.

Q&A

Q: What are sunspots?

★ ★ ★

A: Sunspots are dark patches on the Sun's surface. They look black because they are not as hot as the gas around them. The largest sunspots cover an area 150 times bigger than Earth.

ZOOM

CANDLE POWER

An area of the Sun's surface the size of a postage stamp shines with the power of one and a half million candles! This is why the Sun is bright enough to light up the Earth 150 million km away.

Every now and then, huge, flame-like looping plumes of hot gas erupt from the Sun's surface. These plumes are called solar prominences.

FACT FOCUS

THE SUN WEIGHS 333,420 TIMES MORE THAN THE EARTH AND IS 110 TIMES WIDER. IN FACT, YOU COULD FIT 1.3 MILLION EARTHS INTO THE SUN!

★

THE SUN IN THE SKY

The Sun gives off incredible amounts of heat and light in all directions. Only a tiny fraction hits the Earth, but it provides our planet with virtually all its energy. Without the Sun, the Earth would be almost pitch black all the time and colder than the coldest winter imaginable in the Arctic.

Q&A

Q: What are the aurorae?

★ ★ ★

A: Aurorae are amazing glowing lights which can occur in the skies above the North and South Poles. They are created when streams of electrically charged particles from the Sun enter the Earth's atmosphere.

EARTH'S MAGNETIC FIELD

SOLAR WIND

The Earth is surrounded by a magnetic field. This field protects the Earth from the solar wind, a stream of particles which flows from the Sun. When these particles do manage to enter the Earth's atmosphere, usually at the North and South Poles, they cause aurorae.

SUN'S RAYS

ZOOM

EQUATOR

The power of the Sun is strongest along the Equator, the imaginary line around the middle of the Earth. This is because the Equator is the closest point on the Earth to the Sun, so the Sun's rays have less distance to travel.

THE EARTH SPINS ON ITS AXIS WHILE IT CIRCLES THE SUN. THIS MEANS THAT WHILE HALF OF THE EARTH FACES THE SUN AND HAS DAY, THE OTHER HALF HAS NIGHT.

DAY

NIGHT

SWITCHING THE

Amazingly, because the Sun is so far away, it looks the same size as the Moon in the sky – but it is actually 400 times bigger. Every now and then, the Moon passes in front of the Sun and blocks it out so that a small area on Earth gets dark during the daytime. This is called a solar eclipse.

MOON'S ORBIT

TOTAL SOLAR ECLIPSE

MOON

SUN

LUNAR ECLIPSE

PARTIAL SOLAR ECLIPSE

SUN OFF

DURING A TOTAL ECLIPSE OF THE SUN, THE MOON PASSES EXACTLY IN FRONT OF THE SUN. ALL THAT CAN BE SEEN OF THE SUN IS ITS CORONA – ITS HALO OF GLOWING GASES.

SOMETIMES, YOU MAY SEE MORE OF THE SUN GLINTING THROUGH A VALLEY ON THE MOON, MAKING IT LOOK LIKE A DIAMOND RING.

Once or twice in most years, the Moon goes round into the Earth's shadow. This is a lunar eclipse. You see the Earth's shadow as a dark disc creeping across the Moon's face for a few hours. Sometimes the Moon turns deep red.

ZOOM

CHINESE DRAGON SWALLOWS SUN

Some Ancient Chinese believed that during a solar eclipse the Sun was being swallowed by a giant reptile. But Chinese scientists understood and recorded eclipses as astronomical events as long ago as 1360 BC.

THE SUN SHINES SO BRIGHTLY THAT YOU MUST NEVER LOOK STRAIGHT AT IT EVEN DURING AN ECLIPSE.

11

STARS IN THE SKY

Look up into the sky on a clear night and you can see lots of twinkling points of light. These twinkling lights are stars like our Sun, only much, much further away. With a pair of binoculars you can see almost 5,000. Astronomers guess there are countless trillions out there, too far away to be seen.

Q&A

Q: How do you find the Pole Star?

★ ★ ★

A: The Pole Star sits above the North Pole. You can find it by looking for The Plough, a group of seven bright stars shaped like a soup ladle. Then imagine a line joining the last two stars and follow it out to find the Pole Star.

There are so many stars it can be difficult to find your way round. The stargazers of ancient Babylon and Egypt joined stars up into patterns and named them after mythological characters to help remember them. We call these patterns constellations.

ZOOM

STARRY TALES

Of the 2,000 stars visible with the naked eye, only a few hundred have proper names. Most of the names come from the myths of the Ancient Greeks, who believed the night skies told tales, or from the ancient Arabs, who were keen astronomers.

THERE ARE SO MANY STARS IT CAN BE DIFFICULT TO FIND YOUR WAY ROUND. THE STARGAZERS OF ANCIENT BABYLON AND EGYPT JOINED STARS UP INTO PATTERNS AND NAMED THEM AFTER MYTHOLOGICAL CHARACTERS TO HELP REMEMBER THEM. WE CALL THESE PATTERNS CONSTELLATIONS.

FACT FOCUS

ASTRONOMERS USE 88 CONSTELLATIONS ALTOGETHER. MOST ARE KNOWN BY THEIR ANCIENT GREEK AND ROMAN NAMES, LIKE ORION THE HUNTER OF GREEK LEGEND.

INCREDIBLE STARS

Stars are all huge, fiery balls of gas like our Sun. They shine because they are burning. Stars are so big, pressures deep inside are enough to squeeze atoms together so they join and produce energy – in a process called nuclear fusion – like a nuclear bomb but billions of times more powerful. The star's centre reaches millions of degrees and its surface shines very brightly.

CAN YOU SPOT THE MILKY WAY?

Q: How long have people watched the stars?

★ ★ ★

A: People have studied the night sky for thousands of years. Some ancient civilisations even thought that the Sun was a god. Early Egyptian astronomers recorded when stars rose and set, and divided the day and night into 12 periods each. They also decorated their temples with constellation gods.

THE MILKY WAY HAS 100 BILLION STARS.

FACT FOCUS

INSIDE THE BIGGEST STARS, TEMPERATURES CAN REACH HUNDREDS OF MILLIONS OF DEGREES, HOTTER THAN ANYTHING ON EARTH.

When you look at stars in the sky, their light seems to twinkle and shimmer. In fact most stars produce an amazingly steady light, but they twinkle because we are seeing them through the thick layers of air above the Earth. When the air moves, the stars seem to shimmer.

Some stars seem much brighter than others – sometimes because they are shining brighter, sometimes because they are closer to Earth. A star's 'apparent' magnitude is how bright it looks compared to others in the sky. Its 'absolute' magnitude tells us how bright it really is.

Q&A

A

B

VENUS

Q: How bright are Orion's stars?

★ ★ ★

A: Orion is easy to spot in the night sky since it has several bright stars. Picture A shows Orion as it appears in the sky (apparent magnitude). Picture B shows how Orion would appear if all the stars were the same distance away (absolute magnitude).

HOW MANY PLANETS CAN YOU SEE, AND HOW MANY STARS?

VEGA

MOON

SPICA

SIRIUS

POLARIS

THE 'DOG DAYS' ARE THE DAYS IN JULY WHEN SIRIUS, THE DOG STAR, RISES AND SETS WITH THE SUN.

The brighter a star appears, the smaller its apparent magnitude number is. The brightest thing in the night sky is the Moon, with a magnitude of -12.7. Next comes Venus, which is lit up by the Sun. The brightest star is Sirius. The star Deneb is actually much brighter, but because it is much further away, it looks dimmer than Sirius.

★1 Moon = -12.7 ★2 Venus = -4 ★3 Sirius = -1.5
★4 Vega = 0.0 ★5 Spica = 1.0 ★6 Polaris = 2

RED STAR

THE COLOUR OF STARS

If you look closely at stars, you can see that their colours vary. For example, Rigel is blue, Sirius is white and Aldebaran is orange. Astronomers have found that the heat, colour and brightness of most stars depend upon each other. Hot stars are usually blue or white, and bright, medium stars are usually yellow and of medium heat and brightness, while cooler stars are usually orange or red, and dimmer.

FACT FOCUS

OUR SUN IS AN AVERAGE-SIZED STAR – IT WILL BURN FOR ABOUT 10 BILLION YEARS ALTOGETHER.

★

YELLOW STAR

BLUE STAR

ALBIREO IN THE CONSTELLATION OF CYGNUS THE SWAN IS ACTUALLY TWO STARS – ONE GOLD AND ONE BLUE.

Q&A

Q: Can we guess how long a star will live from its colour?

★ ★ ★

A: Yes. Blue stars tend to be brighter, but don't live long. Yellow and white stars will burn for about 10 billion years, while red stars are the coolest and will tend to burn longest.

HOW FAR TO THE STARS?

Space is much bigger than you can ever possibly imagine and the stars are huge distances away. The nearest galaxy to ours – the Andromeda galaxy – is so far away that light takes over two million years to reach us from there. This means that when astronomers look at it they are seeing it as it was over two million years ago!

2.6 MILLION LIGHT YEARS

4.2 LIGHT YEARS

5.5 HOURS

PLUTO

ALPHA CENTAURI

ANDROMEDA GALAXY

The illustration shows how long light takes to reach Earth from parts of the Universe. For light, the Moon is just 1.5 seconds away and the Sun is 8 minutes away, but the planet Pluto is 5.5 hours away. The nearest star system Alpha Centauri, is four years away and the next galaxy to ours, the Andromeda galaxy, is two million years away!

THE NEAREST STAR SYSTEM TO US, ALPHA CENTAURI, IS OVER FOUR LIGHT YEARS AWAY.

LIGHT YEAR

Because distances in space are so huge, astronomers measure them in light years rather than kilometres or miles. Light is the fastest thing in the Universe, travelling 300,000 km in just one second. A light year is the distance light travels in one year, which is 9,460,000,000,000 km.

SUN

8 MINUTES

MOON

I SECOND

EARTH

Q&A

Q: What is a quasar?

★ ★ ★

A: Quasar is short for quasi-stellar object. Quasars are incredibly bright objects that astronomers believe to be at the centre of very distant galaxies. They are probably the most distant objects astronomers have ever observed.

3. GIANT STAR SWELLS TO
BECOME A SUPERGIANT.

4. MEDIUM-SIZED
STAR COLLAPSES TO
BECOME WHITE
DWARF.

2. GIANT STAR
STARTS TO SWELL.

3. MEDIUM-SIZED
STAR EXPLODES
LEAVING DISC OF
GAS AND DUST.

1. VERY BRIGHT
GIANT STAR.

2. MEDIUM-
SIZED STAR
SWELLS.

1. MEDIUM-
SIZED STAR.

CAN YOU
SPOT THE
SUPERNOVA?

1. BRIGHT
LARGE STAR.

2. LARGE STAR
STARTS TO SWELL.

NEBULA, THE
BIRTHPLACE
OF STARS.

4. GIANT STAR EXPLODES IN SUPERNOVA.

5. GIANT STAR COLLAPSES AND CREATES BLACK HOLE.

THE LIFE OF A STAR

All stars are born in big clouds of dust and gas called nebulae. Stars burn until their fuel is used up. Giant stars swell to an enormous size, explode in a supernova and collapse to form a black hole. A large star will do the same but may create a tiny, dense 'neutron star' instead of a black hole. Medium-sized stars will swell and explode to leave a white dwarf. Small stars glow dimly for a long time and then cool and fade to a black dwarf.

5. COLLAPSED LARGE STAR ENDS UP AS A PULSAR OR NEUTRON STAR.

4. LARGE STAR EXPLODES IN SUPERNOVA.

3. LARGE STAR SWELLS TO SUPERGIANT.

23

EXPLODING SUPERSTARS

When a giant star runs out of fuel, it swells up, then collapses in an instant, and blows itself to bits in a gigantic 'supernova'. Supernovae are rare and brief, but when they occur, they are the biggest firework displays in the Universe. They can burn brighter in a few seconds than our Sun does in 200 million years.

ZOOM

SUPERNOVA

In 1054 a huge supernova was seen in many parts of the world. A star scratched into stone by Native Americans has been found in present-day New Mexico and is thought to be a record of this event.

FACT FOCUS

IN 1987, THE STAR SN1987A EXPLODED IN A SUPERNOVA. IT BURNED SO BRIGHTLY THAT IT WAS VISIBLE TO THE NAKED EYE – EVEN THOUGH IT WAS IN ANOTHER GALAXY.

In their last moments, big stars swell until they are supergiants. Pressure in the heart of a supergiant is so huge that gravity squeezes the star and it collapses in an instant to something little bigger than the Earth. At once, it explodes, sending a bright ring of debris and an immensely powerful shockwave rippling out.

PULSARS

When a giant star explodes in a supernova, it sometimes forms a tiny, spinning neutron star. This neutron star is thought to be the tiny core of the star which has been squashed by the explosion. The neutron star spins very rapidly and sometimes gives out a flash of energy. A flashing neutron star is called a pulsar.

ZOOM

PULSING PULSARS

A small, spinning neutron star sometimes lets off flashes of energy as it spins. The energy can be in the form of radio waves or light waves. If Earth lies in the light beam, we see a flashing light which pulses like the light from a lighthouse. This is why these types of stars are called pulsars.

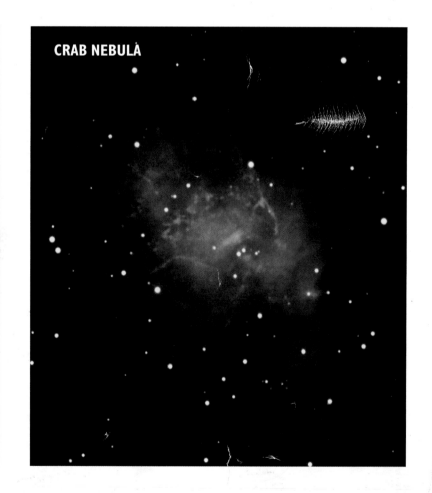

CRAB NEBULA

FACT FOCUS

THE CRAB NEBULA HAS A PULSAR AT THE CENTRE THAT FLASHES 30 TIMES A SECOND.

PULSAR GIVES OFF BEAMS OF ENERGY.

GIANT CLOUDS

On a clear night, you can see a few fuzzy patches of light. Some of these are distant galaxies, but some are gigantic clouds in space called nebulae. Nebulae are clouds of dust and gas. In some nebulae gravity squeezes the dust and gas tightly together, and stars are formed.

Q: What types of nebula are there?

A: Unlike stars, nebulae don't produce light themselves. But reflection nebulae can be seen because the dust in them reflects the light of nearby stars. Glowing nebulae glow red as hydrogen in them is heated by radiation from nearby stars. Planetary nebulae (which have nothing to do with planets) are the flimsy rings of cloud and dust let off when a star dies.

GLOWING NEBULA GIVES OUT LIGHT BECAUSE GAS IN IT IS HEATED.

REFLECTION NEBULA REFLECTS LIGHT FROM NEARBY STARS.

PLANETARY NEBULA LEFT BEHIND AFTER A SUPERNOVA EXPLOSION

THE CRAB NEBULA IS THE REMAINS OF THE SUPERNOVA THAT EXPLODED IN 1054, AND IS STILL GIVING OFF 100,000 TIMES AS MUCH ENERGY AS THE SUN.

FACT FOCUS

THE CRAB NEBULA IS THE REMAINS OF THE SUPERNOVA THAT EXPLODED IN 1054, AND IS STILL GIVING OFF 100,000 TIMES AS MUCH ENERGY AS THE SUN.

CAN YOU SPOT THE CRABS CLAWS?

CONSTELLATIONS

People have always made up stories about the stars, linking them into groups and naming them after characters. These groups are called constellations, astronomers recognise 88 in all. You can use these constellations to divide the sky and find your way around from star to star.

1. Ursa Major
2. Ursa Minor
3. Draco
4. Cepheus
5. Cassiopeia
6. Perseus

1. Andromeda
2. Pegasus
3. Cygnus
4. Aquarius
5. Capricornus
6. Pisces

1. Hercules
2. Boötes
3. Ophiucus
4. Aquila
5. Libra
6. Scorpius
7. Sagittarius

1. Gemini
2. Auriga
3. Aries
4. Taurus
5. Orion
6. Canis Minor
7. Lepus
8. Canis Major

1. Hydrus
2. Pavo
3. Ara
4. Triangulum Australe
5. Octans
6. Musca
7. Crux
8. Volans

1. Leo
2. Cancer
3. Hydra
4. Corvus
5. Virgo

GLOSSARY

ATMOSPHERE

THE LAYER OF GASES THAT SURROUNDS A PLANET.

AURORA

A BRIGHT AND COLOURFUL GLOW IN THE EARTH'S ATMOSPHERE WHICH OCCURS WHEN PARTICLES FROM THE SUN, CALLED THE SOLAR WIND, ENTER THE ATMOSPHERE.

BLACK HOLE

THE REMAINS OF A HUGE STAR THAT HAS EXPLODED AND COLLAPSED IN ON ITSELF. THE GRAVITY IS SO STRONG THAT NOT EVEN LIGHT CAN ESCAPE.

CONSTELLATION

A GROUP OF STARS IN THE NIGHT SKY.

ECLIPSE

WHEN ONE PLANET OR STAR PASSES IN FRONT OF ANOTHER. A SOLAR ECLIPSE OCCURS WHEN THE MOON LIES BETWEEN THE EARTH AND THE SUN AND A LUNAR ECLIPSE OCCURS WHEN THE EARTH LIES BETWEEN THE SUN AND THE MOON.

GRAVITY

EVERY OBJECT IN THE UNIVERSE HAS A FORCE CALLED GRAVITY THAT ATTRACTS IT TO EVERY OTHER OBJECT.

LIGHT YEAR

A UNIT USED TO MEASURE DISTANCE IN SPACE. IT IS THE DISTANCE LIGHT TRAVELS IN ONE YEAR, WHICH IS ABOUT 9.46 MILLION MILLION KILOMETRES.

NEBULA

A CLOUD OF GAS AND DUST, WHERE STARS ARE BORN.

NEUTRON STAR

THE REMAINS OF A STAR THAT HAS EXPLODED IN A SUPERNOVA.

NUCLEAR FUSION

THE PROCESS BY WHICH ATOMS ARE SQUEEZED TOGETHER UNTIL THEY COMBINE, RELEASING HUGE AMOUNTS OF ENERGY. FUSION OCCURS INSIDE STARS, CAUSING THEM TO SHINE.

ORBIT

THE PATH OF ONE OBJECT, SUCH AS A PLANET, AROUND ANOTHER, LIKE A STAR.

PULSAR

A NEUTRON STAR THAT EMITS ENERGY AS IT SPINS.

QUASAR

AN OBJECT IN SPACE THAT EMITS AN ENORMOUS AMOUNT OF ENERGY. THOUGHT TO BE AT THE CENTRE OF VERY DISTANT GALAXIES.

SUPERNOVA

WHEN A MASSIVE STAR RUNS OUT OF FUEL IT EXPLODES IN A SUPERNOVA EXPLOSION.

WHITE DWARF

A SMALL STAR AT THE END OF ITS LIFE.

INDEX

PICTURE CREDITS
ABBREVIATIONS: T-TOP, M-MIDDLE, B-BOTTOM, R-RIGHT, L-LEFT

THE FOLLOWING IMAGES WERE SUPPLIED BY CORBIS —11TL, 11BR, 14BR, 26BR, 28BR, 28-29 .
ALL OTHER IMAGES COURTESY OF SHUTTERSTOCK. FRONT COVER, PAGE 1 — MERYDOLLA. PAGE 2-3 — VADIM SADOVSKI. 4 — KARELNOPPE. 5ML
— AJP. 5BR — SUNNY STUDIO. 6BR — ALEXANDRA LANDE. 7, 31 — MARKUS GANN. 8MC — V. BELOV. 9 — TRIFF. 10-11 — MURATART. 13 —
NIENORA. 14-15 — JOHN A DAVIS. 16-17 — BANNER. 18-19 — BILDAGENTUR ZOONAR GMBH. 20-21 — IXPERT. 24-25 — APRIL CAT. 27 —
MICHAEL TAYLOR. 30 — PAVEL VAKHRUSHEV..